School of Dreamers

School of Dreamers

Written by Fuat Sevimay

Illustrated by Mustafa Delioğlu

Hopefully all your dreams come real :)

Fuat Sevimay
Delhi

UNBOUND SCRIPT

With the support of

teda

the "Directions of the Ministry of Culture and Tourism Subvention Project for Dissemination of Turkish Cultural, Artistic and Literary Works into Foreign Languages (TEDA)"

Translation and Publication Grant Programme of Türkiye

Haval Kurmak Bedaca

Text by Fuat Sevimay

Illustrations by Mustafa Delioglu

First Edition : 2023

ISBN : 978-93-92088-22-3

Publisher : Unbound Script

B-10, Seven Wonder Business Center
Plot No. G-20, Basement, Preet Vihar
New Delhi-110092
www.unboundscript.com
books@unboundscript.com

Price : ₹199/-

Printed by
Yash Printographics
Noida, Uttar Pradesh

Content

1

On the First Day of School

When I opened my eyes, I was midst a desert. I know what mountains and hills look like. I have also seen the sea, lakes, valleys and uplands both in my life and learnt about them at social sciences class. But a desert! Never before. I just know it by films. Billions and billions of sand grains all around. Endless sandy colour and extremely hot weather. Totally desolated. Yes, it seems unbelievable although I am midst a desert. And what is worse is that I have no idea how and why I am here.

Actually, I can guess how all that happened. Soon I will tell you about it, I mean, why I am here and all the dreams of my colleagues. You should hear how wonderful they all are! You may even hesitate to believe in what you read. Because we will wander around deserts and go sailing across oceans. We will become football players, voyagers or scientists. We will visit our past and future. That is to say we have freedom to be where and whenever we wish and whatever we would like to become. Dreaming is a game for us now. And we dream during the class. Yes, exactly. For more than a month we have been dreaming in the class. One month ago, when we first started, we were inexperienced in dreaming and had some problems concentrating and getting into them. However nowadays we have become experts of dreaming so much that we can travel within each other's dreams and we are thankful to Mrs. Ebru, our teacher for that. But first let me tell how all that dreaming game started.

* * * * * *

This year on the first day of school, we gathered at the schoolyard as usual. Girls are busy to tell their holiday memories with excitement. We boys rag on each other on the other side. Meanwhile we do pry at the corner where the teachers are gathered so that we would not be punished since day one.

Our maths teacher, gym teacher and English teacher are side by side. And beside them stands a lady with a dark blue elegant suit. She is probably one of the parents. They have a talk when sun-soaked September day shines on their faces. Maths teacher does not give a damn about us. He generally sets us into groups as the ones who know multiplication table or not and the ones who know the sum of interior angles of a triangle or not. He does not care whether we are naughty or well-behaved. Maybe that is a good point of view. Our gym teacher looks daggers at us sometimes. She would whistle at us if she had her famous whistle with her now. She would then rag on us and say angrily, "Should I come there!" But this is the first day and rules can be a bit stretched. Our English teacher face back to us thus she cannot see what we do.

For now, we can keep enjoying (girls call that scuffle) ourselves. We have missed each other so much and since that Ege nudges Efe, in return Efe punchs on Kaan and Kaan tags me. We would like to be in a well-behaved manner too like our girlfriends but we cannot. We really wish to be calm boys a lot however unable to stand still, thus, please forgive us. Look at İpek and Neşe, they make no noise. İpek stares us and says "They must be crazy." Maybe she is right. I don't know.

Our opening day ceremony starts. Our Principal comes to the lectern and tells that he will make a short, really short opening speech. However, when he starts, it seems to be everlasting. I am about to get the vapours. I whisper to Kaan that I need to sleep and put my head on his shoulder. Just then that elegant lady's glances catch my eyes. She smiles at me. I lose my sleep. Thanks God school bell rings and our Principal's 'very short' speech compulsorily comes to an end. We head to the classes.

I soon realize that I have missed our school a lot when we go upstairs. And I have a feeling for this school year. I don't know how to express but I feel that things will be better. I don't have an answer how that will happen but I feel and I know, we will have an enjoyable year. I really feel that.

Going upstairs, I realize that the lady in dark blue suit was coming up with us too. But she is a little bit slow, kind of having a hitch. Or maybe we walk too fast. I know most of my friends' mothers. This lady is not one of them. I wonder if there was a newcomer student at our class. If it's so, I hope that he is a boy and enjoys football.

And now we are at our classroom for the new term and the lady comes in too. Just then we understand the reason why she came upstairs slowly having a hitch. One of her legs is shorter compared to the other. I think one of her legs is prosthetic. Hold up, we will understand who she is.

"Good morning children. I am your new Turkish teacher, Ebru Bulut."

All the class have beady eyes on Miss Ebru. And she stares upon me. She insistently looks at me. Something is gonna happen. For sure something will happen. And now. She asks me to come to the blackboard, nearby her. Whoops. I am in trouble. This is me who carries the can on such cases. This is the first day, first class hour, first minute. Are you the one to sleep at the ceremony, well then, now it is time to twist in the wind.

"Now please first tell me your name and then close your eyes."

"My name is Kerem. And… how shall I close my eyes?" My classmates giggle at me. Well, we may call it more than a giggle, they burst into laughter. Sheesh. So funny!

"Just like the way you did at the ceremony, bending on your friend's shoulders," she suggests. "I guess you have a talent for that. Then you shall dream."

I close my eyes. No chance. No need to have trouble with the new teacher. But I cannot dream. Impossible. What shall I dream? I really don't know. Then I open my eyes again and stare blankly to the class.

"My dear teacher, I can't. I don't understand what exactly you want. What shall I dream of?" A new burst of laughter. What is it so funny about it? I could not, that's all. Easier said than done.

"Well, Kerem, dream of whatever comes first to your mind, whatever you wish and then please tell us what it is. No restrictions. You have no limits. And don't forget to close your eyes. It might help."

I lower my head from its fixed stare at the ceiling. I close my eyes once again. I really wonder where this will get to. The noise of the class gives place to a deep silence. Now an endless sea appears right before me. I can hear the sound of waves. I have a nice cone of ice-cream in my hand. Yummy. I was about to eat my strawberry ice-cream but just then heard Ege and turned back to real life. "Hey, look at Kerem, he licks his lips." All the class laugh once more. It seems that I will be the buffoon of the term.

Mrs. Ebru asks me to tell my dream and I do. "Wonderful. So nice," she said. Moreover, she asked the class to warmly applaud me. Is she mocking with me, how about that? This is the first time in my life that I have an applaud for having an ice-cream in my dream. This time she asks Ege to come to blackboard after telling me to sit back on my desk. Now it is my turn to enjoy.

While fatty Ege is walking towards Mrs. Ebru, in the meantime asks me in haste, "How did you manage? Is it hard? How shall I do?" He looks very ridiculous and uneasy near the blackboard. We can see the sweat on his forehead with the help of light coming from the window. So, Ege becomes the first student in history who is afraid of dreaming. What an honour.

Fortunately, at last he closes his eyes and when he opens them back soon, tells us that he was flying in the deep blue sky between white clouds. Dream of a flying tank. Now he is the one to be applauded. Oh God! This term has a real fantastic start-up. Mrs. Ebru has an interesting personality. We have a teacher with a prosthetic leg and her first thing to teach us is dreaming. Now she starts explaining what is going on.

"Children, we will dream before each of our lessons for five minutes, just like today. The only thing I ask you is not to be afraid of dreaming. Never limit yourself and instead, push your limits. Literally 'dream' we call it. Following those five minutes I

dream it smells

will be teaching our lesson. And one month later, I will tell you why we are dreaming. We good?"

Certainly, we were good, agreed and replied her all together. So, this was how our "Game of Dreaming" started. We have interesting dreams for a month now and we have become experts of dreaming to travel mutually within our dreams. All the class loved that game.

By the way, I did not tell you about our class and my classmates, right? Now I will instantly. Actually, there is not much extraordinary things I can tell about. Whatever many other classes look alike, ours is the same. Desks, cabinets, teacher's desk and so on. We are twenty-one kids. Eleven girls and ten boys. I like all of them. Even Ege "the zippy" and his buddy Efe. We call Ege "the zippy" because he can't stand still without jumping around. He is even in action during the lessons. No problem if he moves and leaps around by himself however he always tease on someone else with his fatty body. He is always an errant, well whatever, he is our guy. What is strange to tell about him is that, he becomes a pure angel at Social Sciences class and listens to what is told with deep respect, interest and silence. If it is history, he almost lives within that time. If it is geography, Ege almost wanders around those oceans and continents. I told you that I like all my friends but naturally, some of them more. Isn't it so all along? You have casual friends and you have buddies or bosom friends.

And who are my buddies? I already told you one of them; Kaan. My best friend. We have sat side by side on our desks until the first grade and we are also neighbours, he is my playmate and the person to tell my secrets. He is always keen on learning things and curious. He always questions the things that he wants to learn. He is the only person who knows that I am fond of İpek. And he is good at enjoying the life. He can turn the stuff that he is dealing with to a play, whatever it is. And he is also one of the best of our dreaming game. Sometimes I feel like he is more than a brother to me. We have the same taste, similar problems, things we like and don't like are even similar. We are both football maniacs and fans of the same team. Both of us are dreamers and our biggest dream is to travel the world together. It would be wonderful. Our taste for meals is similar. We have no problem with döner kebap and mantı but don't know where to put ourselves when it comes to spinach or beans. Quite the contrary, Neşe loves vegetable and olive oil dishes. She is really a strange one.

If Neşe were a boy and knew something about football, I could like her as much as Kaan or maybe even more. Because she is a real cracking one. She really deserves her name. She was not only crying also laughing when she wrenched her leg at gym class and mocking herself. She had put one of those toys which sound like "faaarttt" when you sit on them, on to the chair of Ege. He is quite fat although he is a hell on wheels. I liken him to a tank. Just imagine the noise when he sat down. The funny thing was, our English teacher thought that sound was coming from a crow. Till then we have been calling craws as "Farting Bird". If I were the principal, I would place a 'Neşe' to each class. She is the exact solution for boredom. By the way, she is a perfect writer. She is a champion of putting feelings and thoughts on paper. I guess, just because of that, Miss Ebru likes her a bit more than all of us and she deserves this.

And when it comes to İpek, she is the smartest of all of us. She is the best of science class and I would not be surprised if she becomes a well-known scientist hereinafter. She is so tidy, sensitive, neat and beautiful. Actually, don't think of an extra-ordinary beauty but I am freaked out while talking to her thus she is the most beautiful girl of the world in my eyes. My heart beats when I see her and Kaan mocks with my scene. Well, so what! I love her.

Did I tell you something about Efe? That best buddy of Ege the Zippy. He is my classmate and neighbour either. Contrary to Ege being so zippy and naughty, Efe is quite calm and helpful to everyone. And his distinctive feature is comprehending details. He is so good at noticing aesthetic beauties, ornaments of a building, colours of an artwork and details hidden within daily life. Once he had taken a corn which his mother has popped nearby his ear and when I asked him what was he doing, he had told me that he was listening the incredible sound of the popcorn. You must try it so you really can feel the soul of the popcorn. And he is so elegant. I can't understand how he and Ege get along so well. The only problem with Efe is that he is really a disaster while playing football. He gives away at least a dozen goals when he is the goalkeeper of our team.

On the other side I am so good at football. And I am the captain of our football team. And I am good at maths either. My friends are surprised with it. They think that someone liking maths is weird. So what? I love it. Sometimes Kaan appears to me like a geometrical shape. I imagine of him a circle head, square body, rectangle arms and oval eyes.

Our class faces to backyard of the big house next to our school and in spring that garden is all green. When the plane trees in that garden become green, sunlight floods to our class through the leaves. And when it comes to autumn, I dream the deciduous leaves are saying goodbye till next spring. The sunshine on our faces accompany our gloom for the ending summer. We get drowsy and a bit lean back on our desks.

It is October now. It has been almost one month till the first day of the school and it's one of those days that we are a bit sleepy and dreamy at our desks. I could sleep if Kaan did not nudge me occasionally. And probably Mrs. Ebru would not let this to happen either.

Just like what I have said. She, perchance, has some plans which would attract us all. She approached the wall and as if what prevents her to keep walking is the wall, she stares there. She probably aims to catch our attraction and for sure she gets it. All of the class wonders why she stares on the wall. And the sunlight which is gliding through the leaves now only shine on her. Let's see what it is beyond the wall.

"I want you to dream," she said while slowly looking away from the wall and kept talking to us. We listen to her as always and as if charmed. The very first week, when we looked at her, our gaze were directly focusing on her prosthetic leg. That seemed so interesting to us then. But now we got used to it and instead we focus on what she will tell us. We wonder where the words she will tell will take us to. Even Ege sits still and listens to her, staying put.

"I want you to dream as always but no restrictions this time" she said and then stood still. She stares at each of us to control whether she got the attraction of the whole class or not. Then she resumed on.

"Our dreaming game today will be a bit different compared to former ones. We all will dream at the same moment. We will close our eyes at the same time and then see what happens! You may dream whatever you want to be. Try to see what is beyond the walls. Don't let the walls or doors to limit you. Dream about the world. Dream about other countries. Dream about other ages and just think where and when and whatever you would like to be. And you may travel within each other's dreams because the one who knows someone else's dream best is her or his buddy. Let's see what kind of similar points you will have."

All the class was so silent. And it was Kaan who broke the silencc as usual and asked "Miss, do you recommend any specific method for that?"

Mrs. Ebru smiled and said, "Actually everyone can improve her or his specific method but I just advice you to start with closing your eyes as always. Close your eyes and dream about what is beyond the wall and how is the world beyond the borders. Think of the books you have read. Remind the personalities that have attracted you. They can guide you by your dreams. Dream about what you want to do. And think of each other. Think about your classmates and friends in your dream." And then she closed her eyes too as if she was dreaming. And with her soft-spoken sound which we like a lot, she said to us, "Just dream and don't forget that I will be dreaming together with you all."

I closed my eyes. I still can feel the sunlight gliding through the leaves of the plane tree. First the voices die away. Then the light disappears. I begin to dream and believe me; this is a precious feeling.

➤➤➤

2

Chiper on the Wall

When I opened my eyes, I was midst a desert. I have seen mountains and hills beforehand. I have also seen the sea, lakes, valleys and uplands both in my life and at social sciences class. But a desert! No, never before. I just know it by films. Billions and billions of sand grains. Endless sandy colour and extremely hot weather. Totally desolated. Yes, it seems unbelievable although I am midst a desert. And what is worse, I have no idea how and why I am here.

I last remember myself at Turkish class but now I am under the burning sun. I am near a sand dune. The slope of the dune is full of lines which seem to be drawn by a ruler. Just like the ones on the sea when the weather is windy. Wriggly sandy lines. Yes, I am midst a sandy sea and my heart beats. No, I am not afraid. Well, if I have to confess, I am a bit scared. But let's call it excited more than being afraid. There must be a reason for my being here.

Oh God! There are some noises behind the dune. Strange noises like lowing. I behave timid to check it out or not. But what shall I do if I don't look there? Come along! I need some courage. I slide upon the top of dune. Now I am at the top and look up. Oh! Camels. Yes, there are three camels down below there. The ones you know. They are bound to a stake. It is not surprising. What should I expect other than camels midst a desert! But there is something else to be surprised. There are two tents nearby the camels and some historical ruins partially below earth. Where am I? I wish Kaan was here.

"Hey, keep your head down. Don't let the camels recognize us." Unbelievable, this is Kaan just behind me. He is on top of the dune, just like me and he too has fallen flat on the ground. So, I am not alone. Kaan, me and three lowing camels. I don't know what will happen next but I am not scared anymore. When Kaan is in my corner, I can relax. If you are on and adventure you would like a friend nearby just like Kaan. But how come he is here?

"Kaan, is that you? What are you doing behind me?"

"What kind of a question is that? That's your dream and it's you that wanted me to be next to yourself. So, here I am," he replied in haste. "And now you ask me why I am here. You really are a fancy man."

"Well, you have every reason. What if I tell you there are three camels below the dune and two tents nearby?"

"For God's sake, what kind of a dream is this you put us into? What were you dreaming?"

He seems to be angry about coming midst a desert but burnt with curiosity on the other hand. He is insistent on learning everything.

"I was just dreaming to be an archaeologist and then, oops, now we are here."

"Archeo... what? What is that Kerem? Why didn't you dream something easy?"

"An archaeologist discovers the historical ruins down below earth and unearth them by excavation. You know we have many archaeological sites in Turkey either."

"I would expect such a dream rather from Ege. He is our historian. Still it sounds fine. It must be an exciting and nice occupation but… I would not know, here, in the midst of a desert."

"I had read life of an archaeologist which has discovered the tomb of an ancient Egyptian pharaoh. It seemed so interesting to me. Following that expedition many of the team had troubles and weird stuff going on. I suppose I was attracted by that. Come on let's go near the excavation. I feel that we will really enjoy that mystery and might discover something."

I climbed over the top of the dune and passed by the camels which did not give a damn to us, so we came nearby the ruin. Kaan, instead, preferred to roll down from the top of the slope. He always seizes the opportunity to enjoy. Some of the ancient stones are above earth and some others are covered with sands. There is a dim, shadowy, narrow entrance just between them. Kaan turns back and looks at me while moving towards that entrance. And I look upon him as asking "Are you sure?" There is sweat on his forehead. Yes, he is sure. As long as we are here, he really wonders what shall we confront down there.

We passed by the narrow entrance and it became pitch-dark. To be frank I have some doubts to move on. But our curiosity overcomes our fear. I feel as if I breath the air from ages and ages before. I want to know who have lived here and who have touched those stones. Just like laying a bridge and connecting past to our time.

We move on within the dark from the hall. Kaan is in front of me and soon the weak light which was hardly enlightening the hall totally disappears. Our knees are weakening. Thanks God that our eyes get used to dark and we can sense each other.

We are in a kind of labyrinth. “It would be a great joy to play hide-and-seek in here,” whispers Kaan. I can’t believe that he still can imagine playing. When we turn right, I realize a very weak light that comes through the corridor. No, this is not the sunlight which comes from the entrance, seems rather to be light of a torch. I was right. When we reach to the end of the hall, I see a torch which enlightens that small area.

There are strange engravings on the walls. Frescos of some men but their heads look more like of a dog or birds. And strange writings on the wall that we cannot read. This is totally different than our alphabet.

What’s that? I can’t believe my eyes. There’s someone here who is on his knees and of whose face I can’t see. Is he an ancient personality? No, his dress looks like contemporary ones. I can hear Kaan’s beating heart. He pokes me pointing the man. I really want to grab the torch and run away back to the entrance. But, no! We are in something and must see what happens in the end.

Kaan silently coughs to let that man notice us. You must have heard the man’s scream. He was moon-eyed when he turned back and caught our eyes. And Kaan in return, as if he had to salute the man, gives out a louder cry.

number sought
has been found

"Who are you? Ramses or what?" What next! Are we stuck with a crazy man to a labyrinth in the midst of a desert? We have to explain the situation to that man or else he can suffer from a heart attack.

"No, no. We are… I mean… my name is Kerem. And let me introduce you my friend Kaan. So sorry for frightening and disturbing you."

"Frightening? You startled me. How did you appear all in a sudden? Well, whatever. And I am Howard. Howard Carter. Tell me, what are you doing here in Egypt, young men?"

"I am very fond of archaeology and we… oops, are we in Egypt? That Egypt of River Nile and pyramids and sphinx?"

"Yes, you are in Egypt next to history. Isn't it fantastic? So, you like archaeology, right? It sounds great. Youngsters are not much related with archaeology nowadays. Whereas some thirty years ago, I mean by the end of 1800's it was not the situation."

"Oh, you meant to say end of 1900's, I suppose, since that we are on 2010."

"Ah ha hah, you, young guy. You scared me but also made me laugh. It's November 1922 and I haven't been in underground enough to confuse years."

This time Kaan was moon-eyed. "Did you say 1922? Are you serious?"

I can understand Mr. Carter's seriousness from his eyes which stare us bewildered. After a while, as if he has remembered something, he says, "Enough of this much laziness. Let's go on to work. History waits for us to be found out," and gave both of us tiny brooms. He takes one too and bends on knees and starts to sweep the sand on the ancient stones. And we watch him to learn how he sweeps the sand and dust. He is so patient and precise not to harm the stone. When the cat engraving on the stone completely appears, he tells us, "You take that part and you will work in this part," to show our working area.

I myself in front of a block and Kaan near another, we set to work. Isn't it unbelievable that we are in touch with history? Someone who has lived thousands of years ago has constructed these stones. Even Kaan who was quivering with fear some minutes ago got pumped up about archaeology. He no longer complains and enjoys the column's appearance which he sweeps with every moment. Mr. Carter in the meantime tells us about ancient Egypt. He tells about pharaohs, tombs, pyramids and people who have lived some four or five thousand years previously and we listen to him with great excitement. There have been a lot that we didn't know about history.

Mr. Howard expects to find out the tomb of Tutankhamon, a famous pharaoh. That Tutankhamon has lived approximately 1350-1400 B.C. That means three thousand and four hundred years ago. He has been a very important personality for ancient

Egyptian history but his tomb has not been found out up to date. Mr. Howard expects to find that out and make history. Of course, with our assistance.

Now it is the end of working hours and we can learn that just from the pocket watch of Mr. Howard which shows time as seven pm. We stop working to resume next day. Mr. Howard who takes the torch moves rapidly and haphazard at the labyrinth which we had come slowly and timidly before. Kaan and I are just behind him. There is a nice afterglow outside. It is about sunset. There is someone in the tents that we had passed by few hours ago. Few Egyptians with local dresses invite us to the dinner they have cooked. But they request us first to put on keffiyehs which are local dresses of Egypt. We do so. With the long white dress and some similar cap at his head, Kaan seems pretty comic. Probably so do I. We laugh at each other.

After our dinner Mr. Howard tells us more about Egyptian history. Nefertiti, Luxor, Amon, Abu Simbel, Thebes and so on. It's incredible that such a civilisation has taken place here centuries ago. As if we are in a dream. I don't even know when I felt asleep.

I woke early in the morning. I was so brisk. The air on desert is so fresh that all my tiredness has gone. After a good breakfast we enter the labyrinth once more and continue our work that we had left the day before. I now know the meaning of drawings on the wall. The man with a dog's head is a divine symbol for ancient Egyptians. He is one of God Osiris's son. Anywhere that we clean off sands, something new appears and Mr Howard first tries to decipher those and then tells us the meanings of them. For sure he knows hieroglyph, which is the pictograph alphabet of ancient Egypt, very well.

It is our third day on desert. Now we are close friends with Mr. Howard and other Egyptian guys here. Especially Mohammed, the one who cooks our meals is a nice man and him insisting on me to eat it all at my dish reminds me my father. What he told me today at breakfast was so interesting. If I eat my pancake and three olives at my dish, he says, it would be a wonderful and unforgettable day for me. I listen to his advice and polish off my dish.

I will work on a new column deep at the labyrinth. Every inch of this column is covered with sand thus it will be a hard day for me. Couple of hours with my tiny broom, I clear the sand. Then with a tool which look like a spud, I carefully take off the crust over the stone. It must have been two o'clock in the afternoon when the column totally appeared. One of the stones on this column is a little bit different compared to other ones. It is a bit fish-bellied. My gut tells me that I have to deal with that stone some more.

When I cleared it all up, I realize a shape on it but don't know what it is. I continue to clear the space surrounding the shape and then appears a shape like insect, kind of a cockroach. Those ancient Egyptians are really weird. They have drawn insects on the wall. I have to ask this to Mr Howard. For sure there is an explanation about it.

Mr Howard gets extremely excited when he comes nearby me. He tells that this thing is a "Scrabaeus Sacer" and it's believed that it brings good luck while staring upon my insect like a moth drawn to flame. At the very time I recall Mrs. Ebru staring upon the wall at the class. She had told us to dream beyond the walls. Kaan who comes by can't take his eyes off the insect too. What would Neşe, who hates insects, do if she were here.

"I can't believe that you all are looking to an insect admiringly."

Oh God! This is her voice. Neşe is just behind us. I could not predict that she would get involved in the case when I dreamt of her. We look at Neşe and Mr. Howard looks upon us as if asking who were she. Neşe instead, inconsiderate for us, steps forward and kicks on the insect i.e. the Scrabaeus with the sandal which she took off her foot. That was the moment.

The stone with the insect engravement moved inside the column causing a click. The column moved with a big noise and a space beyond the wall appears in front of us. It must be kind of a secret room and Neşe is the one who first opens it after thousands of years. None of us can say something, dumbly because of the situation. Neşe constantly murmurs; "Was I to do that? Was I do that?" She is not much aware of what she has done. Just next to her, Kaan nips himself and on the other hand stares into the room to understand what is there. A few steps forward we have an unnamed history. Incredible.

Mr. Howard who gets over the first wonderment, goes in few steps. And we follow him. We are eye-brightened because of the golden articles spread inside. Golden chandeliers, rings, bracelets, tiaras and much more. And a column with golden ornaments just across us. And another tiara on the column.

Mr. Howard timidly and slowly moves on tiptoe towards the column as if he is trying not to disturb someone. He sweeps the web on the column and then reads.

"Kowtow before the Magnificent and Glorious son of Sun, Tutankhamon, king of upper and lower Egypt."

Mr Howard all of a sudden kneels down and bows respectfully. And we imitate him. After a while he turns back to us and tells, "We discovered it guys. We found Tutankhamon's tomb," then sheds tears of happiness.

Kaan and I embrace each other and celebrate. Neşe is just behind us. "Can someone tell me who is that Tutun Com'on and what is happening here?" she asks. No, I don't think that we can explain it. This is a feeling beyond words.

Kaan who is inclined to be a king, take a golden sword to his hand. And just before Mr. Howard's yelling "No, don't," he puts Tutankhamon's tiara on his head. Oh no! I just thought that such things only happen in films. As soon as the pharaoh's tiara is not at its place, the column which created the entrance to the room is closed with a big noise. We are stuck down below the desert. Shall we die here? Please, no. There must be a way out. We are so scared that can't even talk. Kaan feels so guilty that I can hear his weepy murmur. Mr. Howard paces around sobbing "King's Curse. It is king's curse" and to tell the truth, this annoys us much more. As long as the oxygen of the room diminishes, the light of the torch sputters out. My knees tremble like the flame too. And Neşe is not even aware of where she is and what is happening here. "Kerem, please do something," she cries with scary eyes. A mask of fear was frozen on her face. I wish I never caught her up in this. But it is too late.

We should not give up and have to stand firm. As long as there's a code for entrance, there must be a cypher for the way out. Although the weak light does not make it easy, I try to check out the shapes on the wall. I have no idea what can be done but at least I struggle to survive.

There are two cat drawings on the block which is in the middle of the wall before me. And there are three smaller cats on the block below. And below it there are three more and then smaller six cats below and exactly fifteen smaller cats on the block which is at the bottom. Fifteen cats on the block, neither sixteen nor fourteen. It must have a meaning, there must be an explanation. And down below the block with fifteen cat drawings, sun is engraved in stone and there is a writing. I show the writing to Mr Howard. "Don't run your head against a brick wall, Kerem. This is king's curse," he says. No, there is nothing as curse or stuff like that. We will solve it and get out of here. Mr Howard who notices that I am insistent, gets up and reads it even he does not seem much convinced. "It says Amon Ra. God of Sun." Sun mentions light which means outside which means freedom.

I must decipher it. What can it be? Fifteen cats and a sun below. And numbers. A pattern composed of cats. Yes, that's it. This is a pattern. Focus on it. There must be a meaning. Two, three, three, six and fifteen. That's it. We multiply two numbers and subtract three so get the next number. "I found it." I am so excited but others don't care much about. They must be angry with me. I would be angry either if someone included me in such a dream. I must handle it by myself.

I look up to the wall with column which is just across the wall with cats. Torch's light is about to die down. The stone blocks are perched cross upon each other. They remind me of the cross we use at maths lessons. And in the middle of the cross there is a sun. Can it be? I have to try. I pray and then touch the stone.

No, it doesn't move. I hit it. Not even a millimetre. An exact disappointment. I punch it greedily. I think that Mr Howard is right. King's curse stuck us here.

The light is off. We are in the middle of terrifying and desperate darkness. I can hear Neşe crying. And I brought all that up. The pattern is useless. Multiply two numbers and subtract something. Oh, what a solution. In vain. I run out of my hope. But wait a minute. We subtract three. It can have a meaning. Is that? Possible? No harm in trying.

I grope and find the stone in the middle of the cross. It is not hard to know it thanks to the sun engravement. And to subtract three I move my hand below. I touch them in the correct order.

Yesss! This is the most beautiful sound I have ever heard. The column's rattle. It's like music. This is the melody of our liberation. Wonderful. Kaan, Neşe and Mr Howard can't believe their eyes. Tears and scream of joy meshed. We rush out of the labyrinth. We hug each other. It was the biggest adventure I ever had. I have never missed sunlight that much although it dazzles me after the pitch-dark.

I close my eyes and dream. We have turned back to Turkey. We are at the airport. On the exit our parents, family members, Mrs. Ebru and other teachers, all the class have come to welcome us. And so many journalists. Flashes. At least ten microphones are handed to us. One of the journalists says, "Could you please tell us the importance of your expedition for humanity." And another one asks, "Is that true that you were stuck below the pyramid? What did you feel then?" I notice İpek when I was about to answer. She smiles to me. And I do smile back to her. I walk by her. I really don't care neither the journalists nor the crowd.

As İpek takes my hands into hers, "I knew that you would succeed," she whispers to me.

➢➢➢

3

The Fans are Proud of Us

He says, "I know that you will succeed. Just trust yourself," and pats our shoulders one by one. Who is he? A brunet man age of forties. His name is on the tip of my tongue. That trainer… the Portuguese. He is a bit arrogant but so successful at his job. Oh yes. Mourinho. World's most successful trainer Jose Mourinho pats my shoulder.

There is a white jersey on me which has purple bands. Crampons on my feet. This is a Real Madrid jersey. We are in the dressing room and Mourinho tells us, "Forget about the first half. In second half Mesut and Kerem will be the playmakers. You got this?" There are other footballers around me. Oh? Am I a footballer? Besides playing for Real Madrid? Where did Egypt, pyramid, the labyrinth, Tutankamhon's tomb and Mr. Howard have all gone? And what about the airport, my family and İpek? And where is Kaan?

"I am here. Cease to gape around like a fool and get up now. Let's show Barcelona who is the best."

"Are we… I mean… Are we playing for Real Madrid?"

"Come on Kerem. You were just like that at the first half too, looking around like catching flies. You better get yourself so that we can play thoroughly."

"But how can it happen, Kaan? Puyol, Messi, Ronaldo and Casillas are all around us. How did that happen?"

"Just do your thing. That's my dream. Did I ask you why we were on deserts and why we were stuck under a pyramid? Now we are in Madrid and this is the match for championship. That's all and all."

"Fine. I won't ask about it anymore. Well then, let's go and play our game."

We leave the dressing room behind and move onto a long corridor. As we approach the pitch, we hear an incredible noise. When we step out of the corridor to the pitch, overflowing stands welcome us. I am at Santiago Bernabéu Stadium and this is fantastic. All the stand cheer for Real Madrid. It is a gorgeous crowd. These people expect us to win.

When I am on the pitch, I calm down a bit. Now I have to remember the matches I watched while I was in Turkey and do my best. Then it is up to Kaan because this is his dream.

I am the midfielder. Kaan is a striker and together with Ronaldo, they are ready for the kick off. Before the referee blows his whistle, I gaze to the scoreboard. There writes Real Madird:0 – Barcelona:1 and the goal is from Messi in 35th minute. Kaan was right. We are losing and we have to win to be the champions.

Second half starts with the referee's whistle. First couple of minutes are played at the midfield. Both sides try to get the control of the ball. To be frank, we will probably have hard times since that Barcelona footballers are really doing well. Their passing between each other turns one's head. But we are also good. The struggle on the pitch is perfect.

When it is 49th minute, I and all the fans had our hearts on our boots. Our goalkeeper Casillas hardly saved Messi's shot after Xavi's through ball. I really can't express the hum coming from the stands at that moment. Everyone had a sigh of relief afterwards. To defend our goal is as important as to charge and attack for a score.

Thanks God we did not have much problem with their corner kick and I saved the ball. Now it is our turn for an attack. We move at left wing. Any moment that we lose our concentration may cost us a lot. Thus, we pass accurately and prowl for Barcelona's fault.

We should not have missed that position. It is 55th minute and we had our best chance at second half. I end-ran with the ball and dribbled Puyol near the corner point. I felt wonderful after dribbling one of the best defenders of the world but that feeling was a fool's paradise. Because next, Pique, another great defender was against me. This time I did not try for a dribble instead passed towards Ronaldo whom I have seen running into the penalty area. Ronaldo was against the goalkeeper and made a great shot but the ball went out just some ten centimetres on the crossbar.

We missed a chance to score a goal but nevertheless, we are encouraged. Now we control the game. I and Mesut start the attacks at the midfield. We try for a score but couldn't get it. 60th minute is back now.

What's that? Kaan sits on the pitch and holds his leg. He was kicked down when he approached the penalty area. Now there is a mess on the ground. Many footballers shove. I am near Kaan. He writhes in pain. First aiders are on the pitch. This deserves a red card. But, oh no! The referee thinks that a yellow card would be enough. Kaan is better now. He can go on to play.

Our coach Mourinho points me out for the free-kick. It is twenty-five meters to the goal and there are six Barcelona footballers nine meters ahead like a wall. Just for a while I recall Mrs. Ebru and her recommendation for us; "Dream beyond the walls." I pace three steps back. I only dream of the ball in the Barcelona goal net. Maybe it is Kaan's dream but no matter whose this is. There is only one thing to be done.

Incredible. Really incredible. Our fans cheer crazily. I lay on the green pitch and all the team celebrates me. We hug each other with Kaan. And then with Mesut. And with my other playmates. Now that we equalize the score, it is Barcelona's turn to be anxious.

I can't believe my eyes when I run to the stands to share my joy for the goal. İpek and Neşe are there too. They crazily cheer and wave to me. There is a banner hanging in front of them and "We believe in you," there it writes. While İpek stares happily at me, Neşe makes a V sign towards the Barcelona players. I can feel that we will win.

Before they kick off once more, Barcelona has a fresh leg. We need one more goal. Just one more. But I am sure that Barcelona players want that so much too.

Now the match is a bit more stressful. Tempers flared. We really got stuck in now. Hopefully no injuries will happen. Both sides do their best and time is passing. We completed seventy minutes and whatever will happen at that last twenty minutes.

Barcelona got a corner kick and we nearly jumped out of our skins. Puyol's header gets out after our goalpost. For a while all the fans bated breathless. Everyone looks at each other to assert that the ball is out.

Our team gained self-confidence with Mourinho's directions from the bench. We should not lose our concentration. A new attack for us. We had a few positions for a goal but they were not fruitful. It is the last ten minutes and excitement is in the air. Thousands of hearts beat. I catch Kaan's eyes. We have to do something.

We take a foul shot few meters beyond the centre circle. It is 86th minute. Mesut backswing and then pass to me. Most of the Barcelona defenders think that I would run towards the corner however I move just the opposite side with a sudden body feint. Two of the Barcelona players forecheck me. It would be so hard for me to spring across them. I feel that Kaan is few steps back to me. I leave the ball to him and rush to the penalty. No one was expecting that, in fact this was something that we occasionally do while playing at the school yard. Kaan chip the ball over the defenders to my front. I control the ball and there is no one left. There is only one second for me to decide. I can shoot and score a goal but possibly the goalkeeper may save it too. And I am absolutely certain that Kaan rushed in the meantime. So, I pass to the left and Kaan is there as I guess.

This is called fun. This is happiness. A wonderful voice. Goooaaaaal! Thousands cheer all together, gooooaaaal! I hug Kaan. I can feel that he sheds tears for joy. He is so happy. We are so happy. We run towards the stand arm in arm to salute the fans. Neşe and İpek have a Turkish flag at their hand. They have hugged each other too. This is an incredible happiness.

Then our coach Mourinho calls us and Kaan and I go to him. First, he celebrates both of us. "I knew that you would do it," he says. Anyhow he wants us to stand on our dignity. "It is not over yet. Not yet. Don't lose your concentration and focus on the game." He is so right. There is still some time to be played and before the kick-off, I remind Mourinho's words, "Focus on the game."

➢➢➢

4

An Invention that Would Affect all the World

İpek says, "We have to be so careful to succeed." I know those words. Mourinho has told that to us. Probably İpek thinks the same way. But what is that white uniform on her? She had a purple jersey when she was at the stand. And her hands no longer hold a flag but rather a glass tube. "We have to be so careful to succeed," she says. And she has no sign of the happiness at her face that she had after we scored that goal. There are some strange devices all around us that I have never seen before. And a strange, chemical smell. The place reminds me the science laboratory at our school but this one is much bigger and well equipped.

"About what should we be so careful, İpek?" I ask to understand but the serious expression on her face does not change. Moreover, she seems to be upset with my question. For sure she has concentrated on something.

"Come on Kerem. Don't you take it seriously? This is a big invention for humanity."

I have to look alike more interested but I really have no idea about what to be interested in. I do the first thing that I can think of and wear on one of the white uniforms. Even though I don't know why we are here, now at least I am adopted to the surrounding. I suppose İpek is up with something scientific once again. Maybe she is studying on an experiment that we have learnt at our science classes with the strange equipment on her hand. I really wonder what those are but I am afraid to ask since she seems extremely serious.

Oh great. Someone is coming. Maybe I can learn something from him. But, ah! This man is either a Chinese or Japanese or maybe a Korean. Those from Far East all look like each other with slant-eyes and smiling constantly. But this man does not smile and seems as serious as İpek. He approaches and salutes İpek. Now he looks on me. What should I do? Oh, İpek, please help.

"Hi, Mr Akio Shindo. Let me introduce my friend Kerem to you. I thought that he could assist us at the 'Carbon Fibre Project.'"

What did she say? What shall I assist? What is that Carbon Fibre Project? Oh God! Mr Shindo now smiles and we shake hands. But what do I know about carbons or fibres? What if he asks something? Could the things I remember from our classes be useful? Go along with you. İpek calls it a project. When I dreamt of being with İpek, I couldn't guess that she would dream such strange things. What shall I do now?

"Welcome, young boy. İpek has told me about you. If you're interested in science as much as her and if you are as hardworking as she is, for sure you can assist us." Is that me to be interested in science as much as her? Stone me! No chance. I only wanted to, I mean, how should I tell it, I just wanted to be near İpek wherever she is but I can't tell this to a Japanese scientist. Moreover, this may put İpek in a tight spot. I have to say something but I even don't know what I shall speak about. What was that? Carbon something? Fibre, yes, fibre.

"Yes, Mr. Shindo. I shall try my best. This is a great honour for me."

Oh, just fancy words. I will try my best. Whatever, it worked. Mr. Shindo smiles and leaves us behind. I must have gone beet red. How can I be angry with İpek for the thing she got me in. This is not her fault.

"I am sorry, Kerem. You must be angry with me involving you into this project. I know that you are not much concerned but we need your imaginative mind and I wanted you to besides me."

Did you also hear the thing that I have heard? Well, at least you have read it. İpek told me that she wanted me to be with her. This is wonderful and a faint smile crosses my face. Does she know that I am fond of her? And does she have a liking for me? Maybe. If then I love this project too. But at least I would if I knew something about it. If I could understand.

"I am not angry with you İpek. Never. Actually, I am happy to be with you. Only, could you tell me what for your research here is. I mean what exactly Mr. Shindo and you do here?"

"In fact, we are not two of us. It is a big scientific team and Mr. Shindo is the head of the project. We try an atomic fission conversion for carbon cells so that carbon fibre could be much more adequate to be used in industry. Maybe I should put it this way; we are trying to invent something much stronger than steel and much lighter at the same time."

"Well this sounds great. If such a thing can be produced, it could be used for many industries."

"Yes, just think about it. Many things in our daily life would be lighter than they are."

"I can imagine many items. Lighter home appliances, lighter cars and planes."

"I wanted you to be here for that reason. You can imagine many points for utilization of it that we can't think."

"Tires. Or gigantic windmills which produce electricity. Just think about it. If they are produced of this light material, they can turn much easier and effective. Moreover, they would be eco-friendly. We would cease to harm nature."

"This is a great idea, Kerem. You must take notes for these and then we have to tell them to Mr. Shindo."

"Laptops would be much lighter with such a material."

"Better if we don't tell this to Mr. Shindo since we are in 1962 and I guess, he is not yet aware of laptops. By the way, sorry for taking you to fifty years before our day."

"That's fine with me. A while ago we were at ninety years before our day. Kaan and Neşe were there too. We were stuck underground."

"Don't mess with me. You don't tell the truth. Oh, are you?"

"Well, of course not. How could that happen. Just kidding. By the way, are we in Japan?"

"Yes. But it's strange that you are not much surprised to that."

"I think I got used to such things."

"It's a wonderful country. If we have time later on, we may travel around."

Now I like 'Carbon Fibre Project' much more. For that reason, I have to learn more about it. As long as İpek is in it, I have to concentrate and be a part.

"Could you tell me more about this project, İpek?"

"Now, I have told you carbon atoms. We heat them at 3.000°C."

"Oh what? Did you say three thousand?"

"Yes. Then we get particles called PAN. If we can succeed to transform those particles to fibres, this would be a wonderful invention. Isn't it great to deal with science? You serve for humanity."

How come İpek knows that much. Actually, we are only thirteen. I don't understand all that she tells but I am still happy to listen to her.

"You are so right. This material can also be used at constructions instead of iron and steel. So that they could be more resistant to earthquakes."

"This is a great idea. Kerem, I love that your imagination is so deep."

Did she say "I love?" You heard it too, right? Thanks God. But there is something that I worry about a lot. First, I have to ask that.

"Well, you told me that you cannot yet transform those particles to fibre. Is this a hard thing to do?"

"Yes. Extremely hard. We tried many ways but could not succeed till now," she sighs. "Thus, we cannot be named as inventing something yet."

İpek fell into a brown study just after telling those. It is obvious that she is so willing for this matter. Mr. Shindo and all the team are so too. They are all so smart. They are hardworking too. I would really love to assist them. But the only thing I can do is to listen and learn. I study on İpek's notes. She has drawn carbon atoms which are examined under a microscope. They are two-dimensional. And many explanations written below. I can't say that I understand them. Someway I remember things we learnt at maths class. Geometrical shapes wave within my mind.

What about studying on the subject at a computer without disturbing anyone… I have totally forgotten. Computers either are not invented yet at this time of history. Isn't it strange? Many devices we use at our daily life and think of them as if they have always existed, actually are invented a short time ago. Science and scientists are really so important. They invent many things that ease our daily life.

Since that I don't have a computer, I may go and study at the library next to the laboratory. I take few books on chemical elements and geometrical shapes and then have a seat. I must admit that they were a bit boring at the beginning. It was more amusing to play football at Bernabéu Stadium. Nevertheless, when I start to learn something, things get more enjoyable. I learn how many elements exist on earth and mines are composed of combination of those elements and that all those elements have different features. Iron, copper, silver. All these have different combinations. Gold and diamond are so too.

I learn that diamond is the most solid element on earth. So interesting. There are some drawings on that book for diamond and they look like the ones that I have seen at İpek's notes about carbon. Look at them. Whereas these drawings have three-dimensions, İpek's notes had two-dimensions. They look like each other so much. Can that knowledge be useful for "Carbon Fibre Project?" I don't think so. Still I decide to tell about this to İpek. At least she would appreciate my effort on the subject. Whatever, I am so tired now and wish to have a nice sleep. Science may be tiring.

number sought
has been found

In the morning the two of us, İpek and I, were seated at the same table for breakfast. Japanese food habits are quite different from ours. But we eat something really delicious.

I had just finished to tell İpek about the things I studied the day before at the library and my thoughts on similarities of carbon and diamond drawings, when Mr. Shindo came to our table. He smiles and then sits beside. Probably she will say, "Well, so what?" Well if at least she does not mock with me. Just the opposite. She listened to me showing great interest. My idea somehow attracted her. After murmuring to herself, "So interesting, can it be," she turns to Mr. Shindo and tells him what I have told. Oh no! Shame on me. Just as I have thought. He stands up. Probably, "That's enough! Get that boy who is talking nonsense out!" he will say.

Instead, he shakes my hands. I take a deep breath. "That's it! That's it!" he cheers then. I can see the stars on his eyes. Together with İpek and few other guys, they move towards the laboratory in a hurry. I really don't know. What was that?

Mr. Shindo and his team including İpek are now in the laboratory for more than three days. And they don't allow anyone in. What is told to me is they have been doing a very important experiment. And I loaf around. It is April and cherries blossom. It's a wonderful view. Japanese love that too.

At the end of third day Mr. Shindo comes out of the laboratory. İpek and other scientists are just behind. They seem so tired but so happy at the same time. Even Mr. Shindo who was a bit worried and depressed few days ago, now has a big smile on his face. He steps forward. April sun shine on him. He raises his hands and let us know the wonderful news. "We did it, guys. We succeeded."

All of the team is so happy. İpek comes by me and hugs me. I can't see her face but I can guess that she sheds tears of happiness. Soon Mr. Shindo comes to me. "You gave us a great idea, young boy. Thank you," he says. I just smile.

İpek then told me that they have tried a new formula depending on my observation of similarity of carbon and diamond. They have finally succeeded to transform carbon to fibres. This means that I had a small contribution to "Carbon Fibre Project." Mr. Shindo has sang songs crazily when they did it. Next day we had a party to celebrate the invention and there Mr. Shindo sang Japanese songs when we requested him to do. Then İpek and I sang Turkish songs and people liked them so much.

After a travel at Japan for a few days which was really deserved, now it is time to turn back to Turkey. All the team are at the airport to bid farewell to us. This is a bittersweet happiness. We say goodbye to all one by one. We will really miss these warm-hearted people. Finally, it is time to say goodbye to Mr. Shindo. He insists İpek to stay and study at Japan but she prefers to study and live in Turkey. Then Mr. Shindo says goodbye to me. After shaking my hands, "Wish you a happy life with İpek," he whispers to me. I am beet red once again. Then they unfurl a big banner. "We will miss you," it writes in Turkish on it.

➢➢➢

5

Eyebrows of Mona Lisa

"I have missed you so much. I am so happy that you are here," says Efe. We hug each other. I am happy to see my friend too, to be here in Turkey. But! Here it seems… a bit strange. I think we are in another country. What is more interesting is it seems that we are in another age. Look at the dress on Efe. A velvet waistcoat and a ruffled shirt. Then there are those men across us. It looks like they have come out of history with their hats and shoes. Is this a theatre? No, we are not on a stage. It is a square within a city. We are in the middle of lovely historical buildings. A tower at right hand side and a big sculpture in the middle of the square. And what have I got to do here? And Efe? What the hell is he in?

"You knew that I always dreamt of being in Italy. Within the museums, sculptures and nice architecture. Look around. Isn't it gorgeous?"

"Yes, Efe, they look gorgeous. And it is lovely to be here in Italy. It was nice to be in Egypt, Spain and Japan too but how would you explain these strange dresses?"

"We are in 1504, Kerem. We could not have wandered around in t-shirts, right?"

"Did you say fifteen and… ah! Are you kidding me? What was your dream, Efe?"

"I dreamt of living the renaissance period. And I wanted you to be in it and see how wonderful artistic masterpieces are being made."

"Thanks, Efe, but what period did you say? I have heard so many new words within last few days and I am a bit confused."

"Renaissance period. The revival that starts in Italy in the fifteenth century. Freedom of thought spreads around people and artists are being supported. So, the society progresses."

"And how did this period start? Is this a decision of governors?"

"No. Just the opposite. Artists and scientists have started this movement and states were obliged to support then. Do you know the interesting point of it regarding us, the Turks?"

"Oh really? What is it?"

"When Sultan Mehmet conquered İstanbul, some scientists and artists who lived in Byzantine flew away to Italy. And people of Italy who are affected by those new-comers demanded free thought and resisted against oppressions."

"This is a really interesting knowledge. I did not know us conquering İstanbul had such an affect. You have chosen the right time period to see something new in the old ages."

"And we are at the perfect point to live this period. We are at Florence. Come along with me and I will introduce you to Michelangelo."

"Do you mean the Michclangelo of the Ninja Turtles?"

"Don't be ridiculous. Michelangelo the architect, scientist, sculptor and probably the best artist of all history."

"Does he deal with all these you told?"

I can't help to surprise. We come near a thin, bearded man around his thirties. He observes the sculpture before him. Can you believe that he is perfect at all those things he is interested in. Then he catches our eyes and we shake hands.

"Buon giorno, young man. My name is Michelangelo Buonarroti. Welcome to Florence."

"Thank you. I am so glad to meet you. Your city has a challenging football team, am I right? I mean Fiorentina. The Violets."

"Football? Violets? I couldn't get what you mean."

While Michelangelo gapes me, Efe says in an urgent whisper to me, "Football in this age? Have you gone crazy?" He is right. I couldn't count that. Fortunately, Michelangelo doesn't care much about it and says, "Let me show you the David Sculpture." A masterpiece that he has just completed to work on. It resembles Prophet David. You must see the muscles, the eyes, the glance. I feel like it would talk and move soon. I can't take my eyes of it. It is bewildering. There is another sculpture behind which resembles an angel also dressed by Michelangelo. I ask him how can he manage to produce such masterpieces and his answer is a proof why this man is called a genius. "I felt that there was an angel hidden in the stone and I dressed the stone just until the angel gets free."

There are plenty of things to be seen here. We walk around the city. We come nearby the Arno River which flows through the city. We pass across a bridge called Ponte Vecchio (which means The Old Bridge in Italian). There are small shops at the two sides of the bridge and artists exhibit their works there.

First, I was a bit upset for Efe dreaming something happening five hundred years ago. But when I personally had a chance to see the masterpieces of this period, I think that he did right. To observe how some thoughts which seem quite normal at our time has progressed in the beginning, and to witness how art and culture was so effective at social life is priceless.

Michelangelo tells us that the Pope has offered him to paint a story indicating genesis on the ceiling of a building at Vatican, the capital of Christianity. He is a little bit hesitant because the Pope is a narrow-minded man, he says. Upon that, “Never mind. If he intervenes to your paintings and finds them inappropriate, you can tell him to deal with his own business and make the world an appropriate place to be lived in,” Efe tells him. Michelangelo liked that idea. I don’t know if he told this to the Pope later on but now, he repeats Efe’s words by himself adding, “Great. So right.”

When we eat something in a small restaurant, an elderly bearded man age of fifties comes behind us. Michelangelo stands up and bows respectfully and kisses this man’s hands. Then they hug each other. After all he introduces the man to us, “My young friends, please welcome Leonardo Da Vinci. Sometimes I feel myself alone within people and talking with Signore Da Vinci in such a time is a big chance.” Leonardo Da Vinci sits behind us. Efe whispers to me his areas of interest; invention, drawing, painting, sculpture, architecture, science, music, mathematics, engineering, literature, anatomy, geology, astronomy, botany, palaeontology, and cartography. And finally adds; "He is successful at each of them." I couldn't even catch how many professions he told. These men are incredible and brilliant in mind.

Leonardo Da Vinci tells us that he has lived in Milan but when French army invaded there, he has come to Florence. This time I am more careful not to say 'Your city had challenging teams called Inter and Milan'. This would be a real gaffe.

While Leonardo and Michelangelo are having a deep talk on arts, we taste our delicious pizzas. When Michelangelo notices that we eat heartily, he says that we should try the ones cooked in the south, in Napoli. Leonardo asks Michelangelo's opinion about a concept called 'perspective'. When Efe recognizes that I was listening uncomprehendingly, he tells me that perspective creates a depth effect in painting. I decide to learn more about art. And Leonardo admits that the techniques improved by Michelangelo about perspective were so important. If he says so. Who am I to object to a genius. Michelangelo is only twenty-nine of ages and his masterpieces are already ahead of time. Efe,

I don't know why but asks him his exact birthday. Michelangelo was born at 6th of March 1475. "I guessed that you were a Pisces. There are many artists from that sign of zodiac," says Efe. He is a Pisces too and I think he tries to take a credit on himself. But Neşe is also a Pisces and she is so talented at literature. Maybe it's right.

Meanwhile Leonardo takes out a painting from his bag, which is not completed yet. He asks our opinions, mostly Michelangelo's of course. Aha, I know this lady on the painting. "Mona Lisa," I cheer up. But there are some differences compared to the one that I know. Mona Lisa has eyebrows. As long as I know she doesn't have eyebrows at the final version. Leonardo and Michelangelo are surprised, Efe on the other hand is a bit angry. Leonardo asks me, "How do you know Mona Lisa?" I shuffle and mumble something. I have to change the subject immediately. "Well… You have drawn so beautiful that even if she didn't have eyebrows, no one would notice." Leonardo looks at me, then to his painting. "No," he says, "How can it possible. Could it be? Maybe. Oh no. Maybe I should try." I guess it sounds reasonable to him. I am sure that he will try it. Efe and I wink at each other.

AA!.. MONA LISA BU!..

Since that Leonardo admires our comments, he shows us more of his drawings. Those are related to human body, things like knuckles, muscles and bones. He tells us that he made use of a book written by Avicenna, a great scientist. When we look bewildered, he tells us, “It is important to know what is in the thing that we see outwards. You have to feel that.” Just for a while I recall Mrs. Ebru who has told us to dream beyond the walls. Now I comprehend better what she meant.

Leonardo tells that he was dreaming of a vehicle which could take off and fly with its own power. When I would just say, “Like a helicopter,” Efe makes eyes to shut me up. Those are the effects of traveling between ages. What else!

After the restaurant, Michelangelo invites us to his home and shows us his atelier. The ones he has completed and others that he's working on are all masterpieces. I stand still before a drawing. Efe asks me what I was doing. “It's so beautiful that I want to feel it and then I shall close my eyes and dream.”

I close my eyes and dream of the place where I want to be at the moment. A beach. I can hear the waves and the blue sea appears right before me.

6

Who Writes all these Books?

When I open my eyes, I am at a beach. I can hear the waves. The blue sea endlessly extends along. And Efe is just behind me. And Kaan. And İpek. And Ege. And finally, Neşe approaches to us. Altogether we are out in force. I will miss Michelangelo and Leonardo. I had a big experience to observe how art can affect our life and society but I think, it is time for a new dream. I don't know what it is yet. And I don't have a hurry. Soon we shall learn.

"Where have you been? I have been waiting you all for a long time," Neşe says to us and she adds that Efe's dress is so absurd. "Were you a tailor at your dream or what?" she asks. "Together with Efe," I say, "How could I tell it, we came from the past. Believe it or not, we were in Italy in the beginning of sixteenth century." Ege laughed and said, "Big deal. I was at older times but I won't tell it now. Just bear two chapters more." I really wonder where he was. On the other hand, İpek does not seem much interested because she always thinks about future. That's fine but to learn how humanity has improved up to our time is also very important to create a better future. Whatever, let's concentrate in the moment. Now Neşe will explain us why we are here.

"Folks, now we are in Colombia and I shall share my dream with you."

"What? Colombia? Does this mean that we are in South America? You probably dreamt of a wonderful holiday with us at this beach, Neşe. What a good idea. Just like my wish. Thanks."

"Not exactly so, Ege, sorry. If we have time, we can enjoy the sea and sun later on but previously I want you to introduce to someone. I think that art, especially literature is so important at human life." We look at each other with Efe. Those words are too familiar for us. Neşe continues to talk.

"Here in Colombia we will meet a wonderful writer. I invited you to join me because we can learn nice things from him and I wanted you to hear those too."

I really wonder whom we shall meet. We follow Neşe who is walking through a path which leads to a home across the shore. I think that Ege is wrapped up in swimming. He can't take his eyes from the sea which sparkles with sunlight. Soon we reach

GABRIEL GARCÍA MARQUEZ

the one-story house at the top. I can see a man sitting under the willow tree near the house. He is forty something and immersed in thoughts. He did not even notice us. When Neşe says, "Hi Mr. Marquez. Those are my friends which I have told you about," he looks at us as if he woke up from a dream. Those writers are strange people. Mr. Marquez, that was his name, right, stands up and welcomes us all. He is a cheerful and effectual man. We will neither invent something here nor play football but for sure we will be listening interesting things about life. We all take a seat around the table. Sea breeze makes us feel fresh.

After laying eyes on each of us, "My name is Gabriel Garcia Marquez. Welcome to my home, to South America," he says. Even his name is like a poem. Isn't it? "Some of my books are published. I have novels and short stories. And now I have been working on my new novel for almost one year. For that reason, I locked myself to my home. I want to tell you my point of view to write and answer your questions."

Isn't it so interesting? The books we read, even the one that is in your hands now, are written by someone when they don't exist. I really wonder how they get started and how that goes on. Thanks God, Kaan is also curious about such things and he expresses what I think.

"Mr. Marquez, I would like to ask something with your permission."

"Dear Kaan, feel free to ask whatever is in your mind and don't even think to ask permission for that. I like curious young people. And please call me Gabriel."

Actually, we all have many things to ask about books but probably Kaan and Mr. Marquez will be much talking at this beautiful garden.

"Thanks Gabriel. What is the start up for a novel?"

"This is something asked to the writers so often. In fact, there is no such thing to start this or that way. The feeling comes and finds you. Sometimes while sitting at home, sometimes within the crowd of the city and sometimes when you are traveling. It may happen even while you are sleeping."

Neşe, Kaan and all of us listen with care. I have read many books till now but did not wonder about how they are written. We definitely have to tell Mrs. Ebru what we learned here. I guess Mr. Marquez is pleased with our interest, he goes on to tell.

"If you have something to say about the problems, distress of life around, you want to write your observations. And if you are talented enough, the story that you would tell comes and finds you."

It is Kaan again; "Well, is finding a story to tell would be enough? Do you immediately start to write after all? Or else are there some other steps?"

"Actually, there are writers who start to write immediately. But this is not my style. First, I imagine the characters of whose story I will write. Their good and bad behaviours, how shall they contribute to the story, how will they express my feelings that I want to share with the readers and so on. I think about all those so long and take notes. The setting, where all those events will happen is also so important. Then I have a plan."

It is so nice to have and read a book but when I think about what Mr. Marquez have told to us, I notice that writing a book actually base on a big effort and ability. This is Neşe's turn to ask a question. Isn't it so normal? She is the one within us who wishes to become a writer.

"Can everyone write Gabriel? Or let's put it like that; can everyone be a writer?"

"It's a good question. Of course, everyone can and moreover should write. Because you notice how pleasant it is when you write. But to make what you write valuable; you first have to read a lot. Any writer you read contributes to your perception. I do read many good writers and each one of them feeds my thoughts.

They give me ideas on how to write. Hemingway, Joyce, Tolstoy. For example, I also read a book of a writer from your country. What was his name? Oh yes. Yaşar Kemal. He has written a wonderful epic. He has told us the soul of a man. And you have Rumi from the past. You call him 'Mevlana' I guess. His sayings feed our souls. You would have a chance to write good books depending on how much you read and observe."

By the way Ege has been sitting still at least for ten minutes. Is Mr. Gabriel Garcia Marquez aware of the miracle he has made real. Ege was a bit more reluctant when Marquez mentioned Mevlana. Things he tells are so interesting that even Ege would try to write something. He is much interested in things told that he asks a question.

"Is everything you tell real? I mean do they derive from daily life?"

"Exactly so. You may find nothing unrelated to reality in my novels. This is a good sentence by the way. I may use it later on." Mr. Marquez pulls his little notebook from his pocket and writes the sentence he expressed immediately not to forget.

"As I have told, you can never know when an idea, a nice sentence or even a good word comes to your mind. For that reason, you better always have a little notebook with you."

Mr. Marquez puts his notebook on the table and then drinks from his mango juice. "It is so hot that soon things on the table may fly. Well, what were we talking about? I prefer to write loneliness and bitter times of people in the society. To catch an idea, I observe people around myself, my friends, relatives and my family. I have to tell their problems with few images, without exaggerating the feelings, as if they're totally fictionized by me. People sometimes feel all alone within the society. This have been so for ages." Neşe says, "Loneliness for Ages. One hundred years of solitude," all of a sudden. "What did you say?" asks Mr. Marquez to Neşe. "Could you please repeat it?" Neşe looks at us to understand if she told something wrong and then says, "Those you tell are so interesting and show us the loneliness for ages regarding individuals within the society." I guess Mr. Marquez ceases to feel the moment and once more lives a life within his mind, repeating "Loneliness for Ages."

"One hundred years of solitude. Loneliness for Ages. Yes. That's it. Thank you Neşe. You gave me a great idea. I may use that for the title. One Hundred Years of Solitude. It really sounds beautiful."

Neşe is so happy to make a little contribution to Literary History. She smiles joyfully. Just like the moment that she had hit to the insect in Egyptian pyramid so the door had opened or probably even more. She drinks mango juice too. Maybe this is another ritual to become a good writer.

It's obvious that Efe will ask something because he is concentrated on Mr. Marquez just like he was listening the popcorns when we were at their home.

"Mr. Marquez, I mean Gabriel, you told us of problems and misery but what about happy moments, friendship and cheerful events?"

"Art is interested in problems. But you're right. Problems may also be told and indicated with irony and humour. I am a sentimental person. I don't know if it is for me being a writer or because of being a Pisces."

"What was your birthday?"

"6th of March, 1928."

"This is incredible. Did you know that also Michelangelo was born on the same day?"

"I didn't know that. A remarkable and pleasant coincidence for me. And it's so nice that you know this. You probably know his life and works too."

Just for a while I thought to tell that we personally met him but then gave up. Mr. Marquez goes on to tell.

"As I have told you literature is interested in problems but real life is valuable with friendship and cheerful times. A good friend is the one that can guess your feelings. If you can share your dreams with your friend, this is priceless. And I advise you to pay attention to goods you have, not with their prices but their sentimental values. The goods you own have souls too."

Souls of the goods. To be frank I have never thought of this. Mr. Marquez is right. He affects and changes our perception of life. To read what he has written when I get bit older would probably have the same effect on us. I will read books much carefully from now on. They will be my valuable friends with souls.

Mr. Marquez tells us more about his last novel, that its title would probably be "One Hundred Years of Solitude" but I will not go in detail of it here. It may not be adequate to share the private knowledge he told us with everyone else. Anyone who wonders it may buy and read later on.

Now there is sunset and Neşe, who has invited us here to her dream, tells us it is time for departure. We had a perfect time and heard many important things about life. İpek tells Mr. Marquez that she is really sad that this nice conversation will be soon over. Mr. Marquez once more replies with a perfect expression.

"Dear İpek, don't be sad when it is over. Be happy since that it happened."

When it is time to say goodbye, Mr. Marquez makes a compass gift for me. What he tells is as interesting as his gift.

"You did not talk a lot but I am aware that you dreamt so many things meanwhile. Always be generous while dreaming. You know that it is free. And my guts tell me that you have been dreaming of a blue ocean. You will understand why I gave this compass to you when you depart from here. Don't forget to dream and try to make them happen. Now please close your eyes and have a nice journey."

I do what Mr. Marquez tells to me and close my eyes.

➢➢➢

KISMET

7

The Magnificent Pacific

When I opened my eyes, I was at a beach again but my friends were not with me this time. I am alone. And then I open my hand and there is a compass there. Mr. Marquez's gift is at my hand and what he has told to me is at my mind. "Don't forget to dream and realise them," he had said.

There is a pier and boats on berth across. A man age of forties waves his hands from a white sailboat. I walk towards the boat. Oh, did you see that? A Turkish flag waves at the pole. This is a nice surprise for me. I get on the sailboat with a few steps. The man notices that I gape around and comes near me – by the way the boat is so small that two steps were enough for him to come nearby – and says, "Welcome Kerem. We were waiting for you to weigh the anchor." I think that when he says 'to weigh anchor' he mentions to depart from the pier. "Since that you have dreamt of being here, you should know us. I am Sadun Boro and this is my wife Oda. You wanted to be alone for a while and watch the deep blue, is that right? I may promise that you will get plenty of what you want. Let's heave away."

I am at a Turkish sailboat and the owner is Mr. Boro. And soon we will set sail. That is ok up to now. But I don't know where we are and where shall we go. I met an archaeologist, scientists and artists within last weeks. I learned a lot from all of them but what will I learn from Mr. Boro? The only thing I know at the moment is that setting sail is so exciting and an interesting adventure awaits us.

Now the boat moves towards high seas and Mrs. Oda sets the sail. And I mill around. Mr. Boro seems to guess my thoughts and "You must be wondering where we are sailing," he says. To be frank I am burst with curiosity. Soon I shall know it.

"Dear Kerem, one year ago that is to say in 1965 we set sail on Kısmet from Turkey. Kısmet is the name of our sailboat. I intended to be the first Turkish to travel the world around by sailing. We passed by Mediterranean and Gibraltar so we reached to the Atlantic Ocean. You know that it is the ocean between Europe and America. And two months ago, we passed by Caribbean and came to Central-America." Would it be ridiculous if I had asked if they met any pirates, especially Jack Sparrow at Caribbean? Whatever, let us listen.

"When we were about to pass Panama Channel and set sail to Pacific Ocean which is the one between America and Asia, we had some news from a friend we really like. He told us that there was a Turkish boy with him and that boy was dreaming of high seas and that he could realise his dream on our sailboat. And he asked from us to take that boy to our boat. In fact, our boat has a small space but we did not want to refuse such an addict and dreamer kid. And moreover, we did not want our friend Mr. Marquez to be upset."

Oh God! This is more than my dreams. At Egypt I have seen a desert for the first time in my life and now I see the ocean. Even better, I will sail on it. Once more I recall Mrs. Ebru. This time I have to dream beyond the ocean. It will be a great adventure. And I should send a thank-you card to Mr. Marquez when we first disembark.

Now our sails are full of wind and we move towards west. Our boat flounder within the blue. While we have an infinite ocean beyond, the land slowly disappears. Mr. Boro tells something like 'haul up' and I ask what is that since I have no idea about it.

"Haul up," he starts to tell, "is the course which you have the wind nearest. Wind is so important for navigation. It determines your speed, direction and everything. You have to be easy going with the wind. How much ever coherent with nature you are, it helps you that much. If your sail is ninety degrees to the wind, you will have the upmost speed. We call this to sail with the wind on the quarter."

Isn't it interesting? I have always thought that you get the speed if the wind is at the back of your boat. In fact, it is not so. It is also so important to know what is useful for you in real life, isn't it? Sailing imply real life to me. And it is time to ask what I really wonder about.

"Mr. Boro, why did you decide to have a voyage like that?"

"There were a couple of reasons for that. If we can accomplish this travel, it will encourage other people. If a man does not get into adventures, he cannot overcome his limits. And adventurers like us must be pioneers. And another reason was to find out ourselves. We can discover some of our specialities and abilities which we cannot notice at city life, within people, at such travels where you are with your own self. We struggle both with the nature itself and with our nature and soul. We will have hard time at the ocean besides the calm days. Sometimes you will just watch the horizon without thinking anything. We sometimes need to be all alone and think about ourselves. So, I decided to have this voyage. Just like your wish to be alone and think about yourself. I hope that will help you to comprehend this voyage better."

Mr. Boro is so right about the things that I have thought. When I wanted to be all alone, my aim was to think in depth and discover both my soul and nature. Thus, this is the exact place. What Mr. Boro has told already began to prepossess me. By the way it is time for the supper. Mrs. Oda has cooked us a delicious chowder. And I learn that Mrs. Oda is German. At the table I tell them about my friends, our school and that we all have different dreams. Mrs. Oda tells that this is quite normal since we are all different. This is what makes us valuable.

Mr. Boro teaches sailing terms to me. It is a bit hard but so joyful. I began to feel like a sailor. The right and left sides of the boat are called starboard and larboard. Where the boat has its wind is called windward and to turn to that direction is called drum roll. Isn't it also very important in real life where we turn and what is our direction?

After a good sleep I wake up. The sun has raised. Today it is a bit rough. We may have hard times. Mr. Boro uses the sail called genoa jib not to lose our sheer. And he also controls the ropes. And I ask him if I could try to tie a lace. Mr. Boro tells me, "Not a lace, we call it knot. Think about it. And you better try it later then." What did he mean? In the afternoon it is high tide. We get down to the chamber. I feel dizzy. Mrs. Oda gives a pill to me which would make me feel better. At night I had a catnap.

When I wake up in the morning, there's no sign of the bad weather. "Good to have a nice weather. Sea is so calm," I said to Mr. Boro. "I am not sure about it," he sighed. He is a strange man. Maybe he likes challenging with the waves.

After a while with his coffee cup at his hand, he sits down near me. "Did you think about the difference between a lace and a knot," he asks to me. To be frank I have totally forgotten it. "Look," he says, "When you have a knot, it must be so safe and easy to be unlinked. Many people think that a knot is something never can be untied. Instead, you have to easily tie and untie. And you have different knots for different purposes. If you don't use the right one, it is out of your control and then you may have hard time in the middle of an ocean. For that reason, I told you to try it later. Or else we could have trouble. But now I will teach you how to tie a knot."

Mr. Boro is a man like a deep sea. He knows many things and secrets. It would be nice to have knots in life which could be tied safely and untied easily.

"Besides," says Mr. Boro after having a sip of his coffee, "It is nice to watch calm sea but we cannot move now. Did you notice? If we don't have wind, our boat stops."

It is nice to lay down lazily but you would get nothing at the end. To be windless has the same logic, I think. The sea educates us. When I tell that similarity to Mr. Boro he smiles. Then he points our route on a map. We plan to reach Galapagos Islands which is offshore of Peru but it would be hard to get there if the wind does not blow. Then we will not see land for a long time. Couple of months later we will be at Tahiti. It's a country to the northeast of Australia composed of small islands.

Suddenly I notice the sound of the sails. They flutter. I started to look like Efe. I care about noises, colours and shapes more, just like him. When Mrs. Oda notices that I incline to this sound, she tells me that it is called 'flap' and adds that it is a sign of no wind.

Next day we have the wind. Neither too much nor insufficient. Just as much as we would wish. When we move abeam, Mr. Boro tells me how to read a map and navigate. I learn to use the compass that Mr. Marquez had given me. When I have a fault, Mr. Boro suggests me to take bearing at the nose. Then he shows me how to do that. If you are aware of your direction, things become easier.

All around us it is blue. The sky is blue and the ocean. When I look at the sky, I can see the sunlight between the fluffy clouds. Sometimes dolphins accompany our sail. They are so lovely. Late afternoon we see the land. It is a wonderful opportunity to make something that I have always wished. I hold the pole and squall "Land ahoy!"

Galapagos Islands is a strange place. There are many creatures which we are not much familiar with. Big turtles and huge trees. The locals are very hospitable. We will be here for a few days. We will rest and buy some victuals. I eat tropical fruits until I am full. We make fruit salad with Mrs. Oda. We talk with fishermen who treat their nets. We are so far from big cities. Here I feel that some of the things we care a lot at city life are really nonsense.

Now it is time to set sail. We weigh anchor and Mr. Boro, after putting a white hat on my head says, "Come on captain. Show us our way to Tahiti." This is a big surprise for me. And Mrs. Oda adds, "We are at your service, Captain Kerem." It sounds so nice. Captain Kerem. Now I steer. Then we leave the island behind us.

It has been one week since our departure and things go well with us. I get used to being a captain. Some nights we have no clouds and millions of stars shine on us. I give them my friends' names. Since all of us cannot be in that small boat, this is a better idea. That one closest to us is Kaan, the one which winks next to it is Neşe. The biggest one is Ege and the one which seems tranquil must be Efe. And the brightest one is of course İpek. I can't express how beautiful the horizon becomes at sunset and sunrise. Pink, purple, blue and crimson dance altogether.

I suppose the nice days are over. Mr. Boro shows me some clouds far away and tells me that they were thunderclouds. Immediately we have to furl the sails. There is a rush in the boat. We untie the knots not to let the pole be broken. The storm which sent an information beforehand by the clouds, finally appears. A horrible rumble and darkness settle everywhere. We have nothing to do apart from waiting at the chamber. Kısmet wade within the waves. For a moment we are likely at the depth of the sea and just then we seem to be at heavens. We are sea sick. The glasses clash each other and are broken. The cupboard doors were fixed by Mr. Boro before the storm to prevent a bigger trouble. And we have nothing to do. Just for a while Mr. Boro has to get out of the chamber to free the steer stuck. He ties himself safely, otherwise he could find himself at the sea all of a sudden. We wait for him to turn back with frightened eyes. We rarely can notice his yellow raincoat to understand that he is safe. Soon he turns back. He is soaked. We succeeded to survive at Tutankhamon's tomb but shall we able to survive here in the ocean?

The storm was effective for three days. We almost did not sleep at all. And at the end of the third day, it blows out just as if it has never happened. Now the sea is perfectly calm. We are all extremely tired that we are barely able to walk. And our boat Kısmet is the most tired one. Mr. Boro whispers to me, "the only thing I want to do is to sleep deadly," and then snuggles on the deck to get a deep sleep. He is absolutely right. Sometimes the best thing in life may be to sleep lazily. And now we deserve a deep sleep.

It has been three months till we departed from Panama. I am a good sailor now. We had two more storms after the first one. I got used to good and hard ways of sailing. To be a part of the sea is so beautiful despite the storms. It teaches us to resist against the tough side of life. I learn that anything hard and bad would come to an end if you are patient and strong enough.

When I look to west with my binoculars, I notice some smudge on the horizon. When I look more carefully, I understand that those were small islands. Another opportunity for the thing that I love. "Land ahooooy!"

We are now at Tahiti. Land of smiling people. I can't believe how everyone here smiles, no one shouts and all people are in peace. The locals of the island welcome us with colourful flowers and put on us flower headpieces. If you ask me, they are much more valuable compared to golden coronas. To show that they are so happy to see us, they dance with folkloric figures. How nice to be greeted in that manner. We give some presents to them and become friends immediately.

White shores, huge palm trees, turquoise sea. It is like paradise. I heartfully thank Mr. Boro and Mrs. Oda. And to Mrs. Ebru who has thought us to dream.

Orirau and his sister Tiare with whom I have been friends with, teach me how to dance like a Tahitian. Hands to right, then two left, two steps back and two steps to front. It's so lovely. Tahitian soul gets me in. And I teach them to play blind man's buff. We have very nice time on white sands. Orirau is the first to find us and soon he catches Tiare. It's now Tiare's turn and it does not take long for her to find me. Finally, they cover my eyes with a rag. I close my eyes to get used to the darkness. Joyful cheers of Tiare and Orirau, sounds of the waves and chirrups slowly disappear. I farewell to this wonderful dream and will never forget of Tahiti. I remember Marquez's words; Don't be sad when it is over, be happy since that it has happened. I am so happy to pass Pacific, meet Mr. Boro and Mrs. Oda, things I have learnt while sailing, to be in Tahiti and become friends with Tiare and Orirau.

➢➢➢

8

The Caravan and the Dungeon

Someone uncovers the rag on my eyes. I slowly open my eyes to get used to the light. I am so peaceful probably because of the time passed in Tahiti. Almost I can still hear the wave and feel the breeze of the sea on my face but when I look around, I notice that I am not in a place where one could be so peaceful or happy. I see damp, dirty, dark walls and a hulky man whom I guess is the one that untied the rag on my face, who now unties the rag on another boy's face. My hands and legs are tightly tied just like the boy's hands who is few meters beyond me. We are both spit-and-sawdust. I think we are at a dungeon and imprisoned. What kind of a dream is that! I never had such a bad time at none of our pleasant dreams. How could one dream that he is imprisoned?

Oh, I should have guessed that. This is Ege's dream and the boy across me is also his very self. This is something you could expect from just Ege. I really wonder what has he been in and how he brought us here. Well, we will see.

"Hi Kerem. So, you are here. I knew that you would, my beloved friend. I am so happy that I have seen you."

"Efe too had told the same to me but we were at a nice square in Florence at that time. What is this Ege, could you tell me? Did you push yourself to such a dream?"

"Believe it or not, everything was ok till two days ago. Just till I was caught by those men called Ilkhanids. Wait, I will go on to tell after that guardian is out."

Ege tries to straighten up and drink some water from the cup before him. But since that his hands are tied, he has to drink like a cat. Despite our bad situation, I can't help laughing when I see Ege like that. And Ege laughs too when he hears me. Then he bursts a laughter. I don't know where and when we are but we laugh in a dungeon. Totally weird. Fortunately, Ege remembers that there is something he has to tell and explain, so he began to tell his story.

"When Mrs. Ebru told us to close our eyes and begin to dream, I first planned to dream recent history, I mean some time like our Liberty War or Gallipoli. But then I thought that it could be better to dream older times like conquering of İstanbul but in the meantime I remembered something that I have read regarding Mevlana The Rumi. There it was written that Rumi was much liked worldwide and thousands of people were visiting his tomb each year."

As long as I understand, Ege could not stand still in one dream and even in his dreams he has jumped from one to another.

"Whatever, when I just remembered those, I found myself in Konya where Rumi has lived and I had a white dress similar to those of the whirling dervishes. It was the year of 1275."

"Does that mean that we are approximately seven hundred and thirty-five years before our day, in Konya, in a dungeon?"

"No. Not exactly so. My dream started there in Konya but then we came up to here."

Well then, where are we? I may go crazy. A while ago I was playing on the white beach of Tahiti and now, I am at somewhere which I don't know and tied up, listening Ege's strange dream. Let's see what more will happen.

"I attended a rite in Konya and there I was a whirling dervish. You know what is a whirling dervish, right?"

I nod my head and imagine Ege whirling with his fat belly. Oh, it is funny.

"When the rite was over, we went to kiss Rumi's hand. You remember his imagination from portraits, white bearded, cherub, just like that. His image is so enchanting but the better is the things he tells and teaches. He told us importance of indulgence and being honest. Then when the other dervishes stood up, he called me nearby. I was so excited. 'You are not a boy to settle, you should travel the world, you must become a voyager' he said to me. My heart was beating with excitement and he almost felt my mind. What he told next was more interesting; 'One month later a group of voyagers from Venice will land to Antioch. Go and get your place by them. There will be a guy called Marco there. He will be a guide for you to realise your dreams.' You may guess how bewildered I was. Antioch, Venice, Konya, Marco, Rumi. Then I asked Rumi if he would wish to come to that voyage. 'Şebi-Arus is soon for me. I mean the wedding night. I better should be here. You will take your way with them and trail your dream,' he said. Then he presented me a nice turquoise ring."

I was so angry with Ege few minutes ago. He had taken me to a dungeon at his dream. I am still a bit angry but I must admit that what he tells is quite interesting. Him becoming a dervish. Who might be that guy called Marco that would come from Venice? And Rumi calling his death as 'wedding day' is so interesting too. But I still could not learn how and why I am here in a dungeon.

"Rumi sent me to Alaattin Keykubad, sultan of that period. And the Sultan gave me a permission which indicates that I could travel within the Seljukian land freely. And a pouch of gold. I hesitated to tell to the Sultan that Seljukians would have trouble with Mongolians and Ottomans would come into lead replacing them in Anatolia. Then I gave up telling because I did not want to intervene history. After saying goodbye to the Sultan, through Larende which is called Karaman on our day, and Tarsus, I went to Antioch. This part of the travel took three weeks. After couple of days at an inn, I noticed a galley approaching to the port. This was the ship which brought Marco and his colleagues to Antioch. I was expecting an elderly person but Marco was a young guy, only seventeen. I liked that because we could become good friends. I went by him to introduce myself and tell my intention to join their trip. When I told my name 'Ege' this time he was surprised and said, 'Your name derives from the sea. This is so nice.' Then he introduced himself. 'I am Marco. Marco Polo.' Then I got with whom I would travel and why Rumi had sent me to Antioch. What a great chance. I would travel till China with the well-known traveller Marco Polo. Much more than my dream."

Ege ceases to tell and catches his breath. He must have had a big adventure and even now while he tells me he feels the same excitement. Then he goes on to tell.

"Then I told Marco Polo that I would like to attend their trip and showed Sultan's edict which I thought would be helpful to affect him. He had to ask his elders. After asking to his uncle, he told me that they had decided to have me on the trip with them and I could be a translator for them. I was a champ at the bit. And when Marco told me that on their way from Antioch to China, at many places people talked Turkish, I was really surprised."

Good heavens, when I was on the ocean, Ege too have been in a great adventure. We are talking about traveling with Marco Polo. Where they have been, what they have seen, all of those must have been a great joy. Now he continues to tell.

"Soon after we made preparations for a few days and then started our trip with a historical caravan. Camels, horses and mules. Voyages of old times are not like the ones of our day. First, we came to Antep. At that time the city was called Ayıntap. We ate delicious kebab and baklava. I really enjoyed the meal and dreamt of having a restaurant when I grow up. And I learnt that Antep was one of the oldest cities established on earth. Then we headed to Urfa. We visited Pool of Abraham. We met with so interesting people and saw many interesting sites. I taught Turkish to Marco during our trip and he thought Italian to me with Venice dialect. Few weeks later we reached Tebriz after climbing over huge mountains. And then Isfahan where architecture was so impressive. People who were living at those cities we pass by were so solicitous about us since it was not a common thing for someone from Venice being in Isfahan at those days. They asked hundreds of questions to us. What kind of people were living in Venice, how were the governors, what people ate and their dresses, attitudes, behaviours, what they read and the language they speak and so on. Marco was so good at communicating with people and had attractive answers to what people wanted to learn. Sultans, viziers and beys who hosted us at their palaces or mansions immediately liked him. They all trusted him and requested him to visit them when he turns back from China. And he introduced me as his assistant."

Assistant of Marco Polo. It really sounds fantastic.

"By the way Marco's uncle was expecting to earn money during that voyage. They really know how to trade. They bought many rugs and carpets from Iran and sent them to Venice with one of their colleagues. Marco told me that they would make good money of this deal and he also liked trading. I instead told him to think big. Upon my advice that he could be an ambassador for Kublai Han at China, he thought that I was mocking. But I was sure that then he found this advice reasonable and started to think about it. I was an eye-witness to his relations with Sultans and Beys and he would really enjoy and be successful at such a position."

I listen to things Ege tells like a tale. A tale which was real ages ago. Things would be much better if my hands were not tied. I feel my legs are getting numb. I shuffle a bit and then go on to listen.

"After Isfahan there was desert. We were telling the things we know to each other with Marco. He thought that I was mocking him when I told that he could see some inventions in China which are not known in Europe at that time. Then we came to lands and cities where Turkmenistan Uzbekistan takes place in our day. Back then the region was called Turkistan in total and a Turkish state called Altın Orda was in charge. Our joyful voyage ceased when we heard that Mongolian armies from east were on an expedition to this land. People living there were also in a panic since that Mongolians were ravaging the cities they captured. We observed this terrible situation clearly at Bokhara where we were ten days ago. The city which was a wealthy one fifty years ago and where many scientists lived, was looted by Genghis Khan at

1220 and was ruined. Marco Polo was surprised to learn that the famous scientist Avicenna was also from Bokhara. And I have heard that name for the first time and was surprised too when I learned that this Turkish scientist's books called The Book of Healing and The Canon of Medicine were basic medical texts in Europe. And Marco bought some of the hand-writings of Avicenna."

Wait a minute! This name, Avicenna, sounds so familiar to me. I got it. Michelangelo has told us about him when we were in Florence with Efe. I am a bit ashamed of not knowing such an important scientist. Ege does not know either. Actually, we had so many scientists that has lived worldwide. Ege goes on to tell a bit depressed compared to his former mood.

"We could see the signs of Mongolian assault on the buildings and madrasahs where Avicenna and many other scientists worked. I once more hated wars whit what I witnessed in Bokhara directly how harmful wars could be and how absurd it was to make a war instead of dealing with science and humanity. And unfortunately, bad things which happened seven hundred years ago goes on at our day."

It's obvious that Ege was terribly affected with war and aggression. He is right. We think that humanity had a big progress but still some people make wars and some countries go on to exploit and colonize others. Then I was wrong about Ege. Coincidently he has fallen into the Mongolian expedition and somehow, he was imprisoned in this in dungeon.

"We discussed whether to go on or not in Bokhara. Marco's uncle told that he really wanted to trace Afrasiab in Samarkand. He did not want to miss that opportunity when we were so near. And when I asked who was Afrasiab, they told some names like Alp-er Tunga, Tall Ihsan Efendi and Shahnameh but I did not know them. Then we decided to continue our trip. But I was so scared to come across the Mongolians. Four days ago, we departed from Bokhara. When we were moving towards Samarkand through valleys, hundred horsemen hi-jacked us as our caravan swooped around a valley. They were Ilkhanid. First, they asked from where we were coming and to where we would go. When they learned that we were heading to Kublai Khan's palace, they did not give us a big trouble. They just appropriated few horses from us and asked for some gold as tax. Then they let us go."

Well, they have let them go. So why then we are in a dungeon in danger at the moment? And why are we tied? Where is Marco Polo? Did Ege do something bad? Certainly, there is an explanation for all those.

"Just when we were to get rid of those bandits, one of them who had a brutal look and ugly moustache asked me to give the turquoise ring on my finger. This was not a polite request since he was nudging me with his sword. I told him that it was a gift from Rumi and I would never give that to him. He caught me by my throat. Marco was pleading to chef to let me go and was telling me to give the ring. He said, 'Or else they will kill you.' Just at that moment I went crazy and started to scream."

I know the times when he is crazy and you would never want to be there at those times. Even now when he remembered that moment, I can see the stars in his eyes. Obviously, he had been so angry then.

"I told them that they had to cut my finger to get the ring and that their invasions and killing innocent people were inhuman and vile. Marco was staring at me with anxiety, afraid of something bad to happen. I suppose I had gone too far. Finally, their chef nervously told the rest to leave but that I would stay with them and maybe that I would come to my sense if I am imprisoned in a dungeon. Marco begged them to leave me and offered to give some more horses or camels but it was useless. The bandits tied me and put me in this dungeon. And that's all."

I was so angry with Ege when I first found myself here in a dungeon. Isn't it something to get angry about? After the shore in Tahiti, a dark dungeon in Central Asia would make everyone upset. But when I heard what he tells, his resistance against cruelty, I was proud of him. He is fine boy to think this way. But I still cannot understand one thing. Why did he want me to come?

"Ege, you had a really bad time. But I cannot understand one thing. Why on earth did you want me to come? What can I do for you and for myself?"

"When we were in Colombia with Mr. Marquez, you suddenly had disappeared. When we were talking with Kaan about where you could have gone, he told me that in any case, even if there is a trouble, you would fend for yourself and how you had got rid of the labyrinth in Egypt. And he added that if one of us was in trouble, you would be the right person to be dreamt aside. And I thought to myself when I was put in this dungeon, you could come, rescue me and get out of this trouble."

"Oh thanks. Do I seem like a member of a search and rescue team?"

"You have any reason to be mad, Kerem. I promise to buy strawberry ice-cream for you and for all the class if we get out of here. You must have a solution. Kaan told me like that."

"Well then, it would be better if Kaan comes and gets you out of this."

Oh God! I did not expect this. Kaan is just across me, his hands are tied too and he gapes at me. Was I the one who wished him here or Ege?

"What is happening and where am I? Why am I tied?" Kaan seems to have endless questions. "Kerem, Ege, is that you? What kind of a dream is that? Or is it real? What did you do to cause us imprisoned?"

"You have told Ege that I could get anyone out from a trouble. When we were just talking on this, poof, you're here."

"Ah yes. I remember that I have told something like that. In Colombia, I suppose. But, why are we tied? Where are we? How shall we get out of this? Are there any chippers or sort of such thing on the walls?"

Should we tell all the story to Kaan from the beginning? Or it would be much better to find a solution just for the "how shall we get out of this" question.

"Ege, Kaan, come near me. I have a plan to get out of here."

Their eyes sparkle. They slide along curiously on their knees. When they are close enough, I whisper my plan.

"I will count down from three to one and at the same moment we will dream that three of us are out of this dungeon and we are free. We will run away with force. If we can dream altogether, we can succeed. Understood?"

They nod their heads but a bit surprised probably since they were expecting something more complicated. Whereas sometimes to think simple is the best.

"Oooone, twoooo, threeee."

That's it. With a roar we rush out of the dungeon, crossing deep ditches, scaling stone walls. Our hands and legs are free. It is priceless to be free. But it is a bit early to celebrate freedom because there are at least ten soldiers behind us. They ask each other how we came out and stare upon us unbelievingly. When one of them comes over his astonishment, "Seize the boys. Hunt down them!" he cries out.

We immediately have to do something or else we will be turned back to that dungeon in no time flat. "Run awaaaay!" I exclaimed. Somewhere in old Turkistan, Ege, Kaan and I run side by side kicking up. Despite his weight, Ege is the fastest one. It's obvious that he wants to get rid of here as soon possible. And ten soldiers behind, try to catch us, running crazily. They are faster than us and the distance between us decreases. We run to freedom breathlessly.

➢➢➢

9

Power of the Nature Power of the Dream

We run breathlessly. I will almost tear my heart out. I have no more power to stand. There is a big curtain in front of us. It is a thick, velvet curtain and we can get rid of the bandits to save our lives if we can reach ahead of it. I half-open the curtain and we go ahead to the bitter end. One last step and we hear an applause. Many people applaud us. What? And why? Since that we ran away from the bandits? I don't know. I guess I missed something. Whatever, I am sure that we got rid of the bandits. Then the applause ceases and those who applaud a while ago stare on us oddly. There is something strange but I could not understand.

We are at an open area. It is a kind of ceremony I suppose. But not like the ones at the school. It is a bigger, more crowded one. There are flags and streamers all around. And there is a stage which we are on at the moment. I mean myself, Ege and Kaan are on stage. There is also a speech stand on the stage like the ones that our principal makes his speech at, but this time it is someone else to speak. She is Neşe. The one and only Neşe.

Yes, it is Neşe on the stage but, how could I express, she seems older, around thirties. She stares us. And we stare at each other too. It's incredible. Ege is also at his thirties and Kaan too. What about me? Am I age of thirty too? Yes, exactly. We have suits on us. When did we grow older? I poke Kaan and ask him, "Hey buddy, is it your dream?"

"No. I didn't understand what's happening either," answered Kaan quickly. Then I look at Ege. It must be his doing for sure. He probably wanted to grow up immediately when he was scared in dungeon.

"Ege, tell me the truth. Is it your dream?"

He too gazes around and says, "To be honest, I have no idea of what's happening."

While people were trying to understand why we came to the stand running, I approached Neşe and asked her whispering, "What's happening, Neşe? Whose dream is that yours?" Neşe signifies an elegant lady age of fifties at the ceremony and "I suppose we are in Mrs. Ebru's dream," she explains to me. Oh

God. My teacher smiles at me just across. She is a little bit older but still so beautiful. I bow my head to greet her and she in return greets us.

Neşe tells us to step back since that she will have her speech. She adjusts the microphone and starts to talk.

"Dear guests. Today we gathered here for the opening ceremony of 'İstanbul Energy Project'. You're all welcome."

While people clap enthusiastically, I look up at the scene beyond us. Incredible. I couldn't notice them in excitement till now. More than fifty wind power plants are up there at the slope of a mountain. Just like the ones we have dreamt with İpek when we were at Japan. Huge windmills which produce electricity. I don't know who has constructed them but they seem like huge fantastic toys. Neşe continues her speech.

"Actually, this project dates to seventeen years back. The first kick-off was at Tall Ihsan Efendi School, at Mrs. Ebru's class."

Who is that Tall Ihsan Efendi? He is once more in our story. I had heard of him once more some time ago. As our school is named after him, apparently, he must be a personage. Whatever, let's listen to Neşe.

"Our friendship depending to those years got along with the dreaming talent Mrs. Ebru taught us, so we attended reputed schools and had occupations that we want. Many of you may know that I am a writer and my book with the title 'Our Voyage in South America' will be soon published."

That's great news. Neşe had become a writer as she always wanted to be. She must have written a cheerful and delightful book. She probably mentioned Mr. Marquez too. And what about Kaan, İpek, Efe, Ege? And what about me? The answer may be hidden in Neşe's speech.

"When they asked me to make the opening speech of this project, I gladly accepted since I could also have a chance to see my beloved teacher and my dearest friends. By the way I really don't know why my dear husband Kaan, whom you probably would remember from his sport programs on TV, is on the stage."

What? Have Neşe and Kaan married? I am struck all of a heap. You are a caution, Kaan! While I had told him everything about İpek, he has been on the sly about Neşe! Anyway, I am so happy to hear that. Neşe continues her speech after a lovely glance to his husband, Kaan.

"Moreover, I don't know why my dear friend Ege, who owns a restaurant where he cooks us delicious kebabs, is on the stage.

Kaan and Ege, may I request you to come off the stage. Because I will now invite two persons which deserve to be aside Kerem."

Oops, they come off and I am still on the stage. Why am I here and who will come aside? Once again, Neşe has the answer.

"You all know İpek who is one of the renowned scientists of our country, who is also a schoolmate and dear friend of mine. And many of you also know Efe who is a leading architect of extraordinary projects. Kerem, İpek and Efe united their dreams and carried out this wonderful project. So, I request you to welcome İpek and Efe on to the stage with your applauses."

İpek and Efe who has left their seats among the guests to Ege and Kaan, come on to the stage. İpek is more beautiful at her age of thirty. I hug them both. But why am I here? I ask that to İpek. Her answer is serious as always, "We worked hard to succeed and we deserved it, Kerem. Now let's enjoy it." If she says so. But please could someone tell me what have we succeeded?

"Dear guests. As you all know our state promoted clean energy a while ago which would help posterity to live in a better environment. And it is decided that all İstanbul's energy would be supplied by wind. And for that the light material which İpek improved is used. And Efe undertook the architectural design of the energy plants. And Kerem handled all the engineering processes of the project. He did a great job with his solutions even for the hardest problems and was one of the key factors in accomplishment of the project."

We hear another applause. Have I been an engineer? I am not surprised that İpek became a scientist. I am fine with Efe becoming an architect too. But what about me being an engineer. My mother and father would be proud of that. And yes, there they are, waving hands to me. It is a perfect feeling. I want to hug İpek and Efe to share my happiness but I should wait for it. Because Neşe has something more to tell.

"And now please welcome our beloved teacher Mrs. Ebru on to the stage to share her dreams with us."

She slowly comes on to the stage accompanied with the claps. She hugs and celebrates each of us one by one. We really have missed her. Before starting to make her speech, she invites Kaan, Ege and all other classmates to the stage. Now all the class is on the stage and our teacher is at the stand.

"Dear guests. Our country needs such successful young women and men. And the very first thing that those young guys should do is to dream. Behold, they have dreamt of a life compatible with nature and this is the result. They just have to dream, work on those dreams and then enjoy it. The one and only thing I wish you to know is that, I am proud of them all."

Dear guests. Our country needs such successful young people

Mrs. Ebru sheds tears of happiness. She looks at each one of us so emotionally that we feel her love deep in our hearts. We hug her and she caresses our heads. The scene slowly invades. Now I can only hear the peaceful silence.

➢➢➢

10

Awakening

Mrs. Ebru caresses our heads and says, "Come on lads, it is time to wake up, open your eyes!" I open my eyes. We are at our class where all this had begun. The class is so silent that I can feel the peace in the silence. Sunlight floods to our class through the leaves of the plane trees. Kaan, İpek and all the class open their eyes. Everyone looks at each other. Everyone has a nice smile on their face. We try to understand if we are still in a dream or turned back to reality. Mrs. Ebru smiles. Her smile is too real to be dreamt.

"Well, tell me. What have you been dreaming? Where have you been? Who is the first?"

She looks at me. She keeps looking. Well, that means I am the one to tell it first. I tell them Egypt, Mr. Howard, the labyrinth, how we found Tutankhamon's tomb. I tell in detail the chipper on the wall and how we got out of the pyramid. "It's so lovely and interesting," said Mrs. Ebru. Neşe tells that she had felt as if she was there too. We smile to each other with Kaan.

Then a friend of us told that she was a musician in Vienna and another one has been a doctor in Turkey. All the dreams are so beautiful. It's İpek's turn to tell. She talks about the 'Carbon Fibre Project'. She tells Mr. Shindo and that important invention. And when she said, "Kerem was in my dream too," Kaan started to giggle and I had a flush on my face.

There have been friends who dreamt of becoming a veterinarian or travel around Europe after becoming a machinist. One of our friends has dreamt of becoming a pasha during the period of Suleiman the Magnificent. After him telling the events he was in, it's Efe's turn and he says, "I dreamt the same period but I was at Italia with Michelangelo," and he tells us about David, Mona Lisa and all other artistic movements.

Neşe tells us Mr. Marquez, his books, her dream of becoming a writer and that some of us were too. When I listen to Neşe, I put my hand to my pocket. There is a compass there. I put it back before anyone can see it.

One of our friends has been a captain and has saved Titanic before it crashes to the iceberg. I remind Mr. Boro and Mrs. Oda, our boat Kısmet, the white clouds, dolphins and the Pacific. I remember Tahiti, my friends Tiare and Orirau. I wish they were here. How nice would that be.

"Hi Kerem. Is it your country? Are we in your class? Are these your friends?" interrupts a voice. That must be a miracle. Tiare and Orirau stand next to me in our class. I introduce them to all my classmates and then tell my adventure on Pacific. That the sea there was turquoise and that there was a peace in the breeze. Upon that Neşe says, "I also remember something about wind but the details are shadowy. I suppose I had a speech on stage but the rest of the dream is gone." Then Mrs. Ebru smiles and tells us about her dream. At her dream we had different occupations. When she tells that Kaan was a sports anchor, Kaan tells his dream about playing football with Real Madrid in Spain.

One of our friends has pushed the limits and have been at prehistoric ages with dinosaurs. But at the end he had to run away from the dinosaurs and even now he is a bit frightened with sweat on his forehead.

There is only Ege left who has not told his dream. After telling Konya, Rumi, Marco Polo and his voyage, he says, "I had to escape at the end of my dream and I have to thank Kerem since he saved me there and I should buy ice-cream to all the class since I promised in return."

"Fine," says Mrs. Ebru, "If you had a promise, we will go the ice-cream shop after the class."

Then she looks at all of us. "Do you remember that one month ago I have told Kerem and Ege to dream and I have said this would continue at each class? And I have also promised to cxplain why we do something like that after a while. Now today, I want to tell you the reason."

Mrs. Ebru taught us how to think. She always tells us how valuable education is. She has taught us how to question and analyse things, importance of justice and claiming our rights. To dream, wonder about things, being courageous, to enjoy life. When she comes to the class, we all feel happy. She can guess if one of us is bothered. Within one month our class became a more enjoyable place.

"Dear lads. When I was eight years old, which means five years younger than your current age, we had a terrible accident while we were traveling to visit some relatives in Bursa. My parents and brother were slightly wounded but my arm and leg were broken and badly injured. I suffered a big pain and I

remember that besides crying, I was thinking that things would never be happily the same for me. I had few surgeries. My arm slowly recovered but I could not tell the same for my leg. I could not attend the school that year and one day, the doctor told us some worse news. My leg had to be cut. I felt terrible."

We were listening what Mrs. Ebru has lived through that time as if living personally. For a moment I really felt a pain at my leg. She must have suffered so much. None of us had courage to ask why her leg was prosthetic up till now. Maybe we were used to it. But what can be the relation of all those with our dreaming game? Here comes the answer from Mrs. Ebru.

"Then my leg was cut. I never wanted to talk to anyone and day by day I was turning in on myself. My parents were probably sad about my emotional state more than the accident. My teacher who was visiting me each week at that time was also very upset and one day he had a magazine at his hand. There was an article which told that a young guy who had gone blind after a similar accident of mine, then he had become a maths professor. This was a victory of determination and devotion. An article at another newspaper he brought next week was about a mentally challenged girl who had invented a very productive process at cattle breeding due to her extraordinary relation with the animals. Then some news about daughter of a very poor family with six children who had great success later on at business life, another man who has succeeded to peak Mount Ararat. This had turned to a play for us and I was expecting the news that my teacher would bring to me with a big excitement. And my schoolmates also got into this play and they brought similar news and stories to me each week.

When I was not as desperate as former days, my teacher asked me to dream. He said, 'Don't bother about your leg. There are plenty of things that you can despite your disability. Just dream about them, Ebru, and tell me.' After thinking about it couple of days, I told him that I dreamt of three things. The first one was to have a prosthetic leg. Then to become a teacher full of love just like him. And finally, to teach my students in the future the beauty of dreaming and believing in those dreams."

Mrs. Ebru's eyes are sparkling now. And to look at those eyes motivates us all.

"My first two dreams became real. And the third one is realising with your help. And I ask you to dream always in your life. Nothing starts without dreaming. To want and to have an effort is so important but you cannot know exactly what you want if you don't dream. Even worse you may work for others; your effort may be just for their dreams and you may fall apart from your own dreams. Instead, if you dream, you know what you want from life. Many things that are assumed to be impossible have become real through the dreams of some pioneers. And never forget, it is of the greatest importance, which is free to dream."

We promise Mrs. Ebru that we will never cease to dream and use our efforts to realise them.

The school bell rings. It is the break. We leave the school yard and go to the ice-cream shop at the next street. There the ice-cream is made of fruit and milk and not like the sloppy ones sold at the markets. Ege buys for all of us. Tiare tells that it was the best ice-cream she ever ate. By the way I notice a turquoise ring at Tiare's finger which she holds the cone. I suppose that we will have Tahitian food at Ege's restaurant in near future.

The strawberry ice-cream is delicious. Do you long for it too? Just dream that you have a big cone at your hand and eat it. You can feel the taste, right?